Around Town

I Talk You Talk Press

ISBN: 978-4-910971-09-4

www.italkyoutalk.com

info@italkyoutalk.com

CONTENTS

I Talk You Talk Press

INTRODUCTION

Glasstown is a small town in the north of England. It is a friendly town. It has around 50,000 people. It is famous for making glass. A long time ago, there were many glass-making factories. It is also famous for rugby. The town's rugby team is very good. They win many games and tournaments.

On the main street, there are shops, restaurants, a bank, a library, a clinic, and a hair salon. The people in Glasstown like to go to the main street to go shopping or to talk to other people.

In this book, there are five stories about places in Glasstown.

1. THE RESTAURANT

Terry is excited. Tonight, there is a big event in his restaurant. The local government members are going to have a meeting with the managers of a big company. The company wants to build an IT centre in Glasstown. This is good for the town. There are not many jobs in Glasstown. If the company builds an IT centre, there will be 200 new jobs.

Terry is also nervous. *If the managers don't like the food, maybe they won't build their IT centre in Glasstown,* he thinks.

There are two restaurants in Glasstown. Terry's restaurant is a local food restaurant. It has fish and chips, pies, and meat and vegetable dishes. The other restaurant is an Italian restaurant. Terry's restaurant is very old. His mother and father opened the restaurant 50 years ago. A man from the local government said to Terry, "Your restaurant has a long history in Glasstown. We want to show the managers of the IT company our history and tradition. So, we want to take them to your restaurant."

It is the morning of the meeting. Terry goes into the kitchen of the restaurant. For the meeting, he is going to make roast beef, roast potatoes and vegetables. He switches the gas cooker on. But there is a problem. The gas cooker is broken.

Oh no! thinks Terry. *Tonight is very important! If the gas cooker is broken, I can't cook anything! I will call a repair person.*

Terry calls a repair company. After thirty minutes, a repairman comes.

"So, you have a problem with your gas cooker?" he asks Terry.

"Yes, I do," says Terry. "Can you fix it?"

"I'll try my best," says the man. He goes into the kitchen and looks at the cooker. After five minutes, he says to Terry, "I'm sorry. I can't fix it. It needs a new part. I have to order the new part. I can fix it next week."

"Next week?" says Terry. "But I need my cooker today! I have very important customers this evening!"

"I'm sorry," says the man. "I can't fix it today."

The man leaves. Terry sits down in his restaurant. *What am I going to do?* he thinks. *I have to call the government. But they will be angry. The meeting this evening is very important. If they cancel the meeting, maybe the IT company won't build a factory here. That is bad for the town.*

Then, he has an idea. *The government and the company can have their meeting in the Italian restaurant. The Italian restaurant is my rival, but I don't want the government and the company to cancel the meeting. I will go and see Giovanni, the owner of the restaurant,* he thinks.

He puts his coat on and goes out of the restaurant. He locks the door and walks down the street.

"Hello Terry," says an old woman. "Your restaurant has a big event tonight. It is very important for our town. Good luck!"

Terry smiles. "Thank you," he says. He goes to the Italian restaurant. The door is closed, but he can see Giovanni through the window. He knocks on the window.

Giovanni looks at Terry. Then, he opens the door.

"Terry, good morning," he says.

"Good morning, Giovanni. Can I come in?" says Terry.

"Yes," says Giovanni.

Terry walks into the restaurant. They sit down at a table.

"Is there a problem?" asks Giovanni. "You don't look happy."

"There is a big problem," says Terry. "There is an important meeting in my restaurant tonight."

"Yes, the government and the IT company," says Giovanni. "If the company comes to Glasstown, they will create jobs. It's very important."

"But there is a problem. My gas cooker is broken. I can't make any food. So, can the government and the company have their meeting here, in your restaurant?"

Giovanni looks at Terry. *This will be good for my restaurant,* he thinks. *It is an important event. But…*

"Thank you, Terry, but the government chose your restaurant because it has a long history in this town. The government wants to show the company our history and our traditional food. My restaurant is only ten years old," says Giovanni. "Here is not a good place for the meeting."

"But I have no gas cooker!" says Terry.

"I have an idea," says Giovanni. "You are my rival, but I want to help the town. You can use my gas cooker."

Terry looks at Giovanni. "Really?" he asks. "Is that OK?"

"Yes," says Giovanni. The meeting is important for the town. I will help you cook, too."

Terry smiles at Giovanni. "Thank you so much!" he says.

"That's OK," says Giovanni. "The people in this town always help each other."

That day, Terry and Giovanni cook the food. Then, they take it to Terry's restaurant. In the evening, the government members and the IT company managers come to the restaurant.

"This food is delicious!" says Susan, the top manager of the company.

"It is local, traditional food," says Fiona, from the government. "This restaurant has a long history. Our town has a long history too."

"If we open our IT centre here, we will enjoy eating in this restaurant," says Susan. "I love traditional food."

Terry listens to their conversation and smiles. Of course, there are rivals in the town, but at important times, the people in the town work together. Glasstown is a very special place.

2. THE HAIR SALON

Kylie is ten years old. On Saturday afternoon, her friend is going to have a birthday party. Kylie is excited. She is going to wear a blue dress. She looks in the mirror.

I want blue hair for the party, she thinks.

She goes into the living room to talk to her mother.

"Mum, I want blue hair for the party this afternoon," she says.

"Blue hair?" Her mother is surprised. "But you have to go to school on Monday. You can't go to school with blue hair."

"It's OK. My friend Ella had pink hair last year. The colour washes out. It doesn't stay in the hair. If I use shampoo and wash my hair, the colour will come out. Please Mum! Just for the party today!"

"OK," says Kylie's mother. "Just for the party. When you come home, you have to wash your hair."

"Thank you!" says Kylie. "Let's go to the hair salon now!"

Michelle is the owner of the hair salon in Glasstown. A young woman works with her. Her name is Angie. She is new. She started working with Michelle two months ago.

Kylie and her mother go into the hair salon.

"Hello!" says Michelle.

"Hello," says Kylie's mother. "Do you have time to colour Kylie's hair? She wants blue hair for a party this afternoon."

"Yes, we have time," says Michelle. "Do you want the colour to wash out with shampoo after the party?"

"Yes, of course," says Kylie's mother. "She can't go to school on

Monday with blue hair!"

Then, Michelle's phone rings. She answers it. A few minutes later, she finishes the call.

"I'm sorry, I have to go out. My father had an accident. He is in hospital. Angie will colour your hair."

"OK," says Kylie's mother.

Michelle goes out of the hair salon. "Come and sit down," Angie says to Kylie. Kylie sits in front of the mirror.

"I'm excited!" says Kylie. "I'm going to have blue hair!"

Angie goes into the backroom. There are many different colours. There are two kinds of blue colour.

I'll use this one, thinks Angie. *It is bright. The other one is dark.*

"You are going to look great!" says Angie to Kylie.

"I hope so!" says Kylie.

Angie washes Kylie's hair and puts the colour on. She dries Kylie's hair.

"Mum! Look! My hair is blue!" says Kylie. "I look great!"

Angie and Kylie's mother smile. "Yes, you look great!" says her mother.

That afternoon, Kylie goes to her friend's birthday party. Everyone is looking at Kylie's hair. They say, "Wow! Your hair is so cool!" Kylie is happy. She has a good time.

When she goes home, her mother says, "Go to the bathroom and wash your hair."

Kylie goes to the bathroom and washes her hair. But there is a problem. The colour does not wash out!

"Mum! Help me!" shouts Kylie. "The colour doesn't wash out!"

"What?" Kylie's mother is very shocked. She goes into the bathroom to help Kylie. They wash her hair many times, but her hair is still blue.

"Come on, let's go to the hair salon. Maybe they can help," says her mother.

They go to the hair salon. Michelle is back.

"Did you enjoy your party?" asks Michelle.

"Yes, I did," says Kylie.

"But there is a problem. We washed her hair many times, but it is still blue!" says her mother.

"Oh no. Angie, what colour did you use?" asks Michelle.

Angie goes to the back room. She brings some blue colour.

"I used this," she says. "It is brighter than the other blue."

Michelle looks at it.

"Oh no! Angie! This colour is permanent! It doesn't wash out!"

"What?" says Kylie's mother. "This is terrible! Kylie has to go to school on Monday. The school will be very angry!

"I'm so sorry," says Angie. "I didn't read the instructions on the box."

"Can you fix it?" asks Kylie's mother.

Michelle thinks. Then, she says, "If we change the colour again, it will damage her hair. We have to wait for her hair to grow."

"But that will take a long time!" says Kylie's mother. "It will take many months!"

"I'm so sorry," says Michelle. "I will write a letter to the school. I will tell them about our mistake."

Kylie is listening to the conversation. She smiles.

I will have blue hair for a few months! she thinks. *This is great!*

3. THE LIBRARY

Fred is 81 years old. His wife died last year. He is lonely. He goes to the town centre every Thursday. He goes to the supermarket, and then he goes to the library. He loves the library. He spends around three hours there. He sits on a soft chair and reads the newspapers and some books.

Now, Fred is in the library. He looks at the clock on the wall.

Oh! It's two thirty! My bus leaves in five minutes! he thinks.

Fred hurries out of the library and goes to the bus stop. He catches his bus, and goes home.

I was reading an interesting story in the newspaper, he thinks. *I forgot about my bus.*

In the library, Gillian is busy. She is putting books back on the shelves. She has worked in the library for ten years. She likes her job.

"Excuse me."

Gillian looks up. She sees a woman standing next to her.

"Yes, can I help you?" she asks.

"Well, there is a package on the table in the main room," says the woman. "But there are no people near the package. I think it is dangerous."

Gillian goes into the main room with the woman. She sees a black bag on the table. There are some people in the main room. She asks them, "Is this your bag?" Everyone says, "No."

"I think it's a bomb," says the woman.

Oh no. What should I do? thinks Gillian. *The police always say, 'If you see any packages or bags with no owner, call the police.'*

She goes to the counter. Her boss, Emma is there.

"Emma," she says. "There is a bag on the table. There is no owner. What should we do?"

Emma goes to look at the bag. It is big, and it looks heavy.

"We should call the police," she says.

Emma picks up the phone and calls the police.

"Hello. This is Glasstown Library," she says. "There is a bag in the library, but it has no owner."

"We will come to the library now," says the police officer. "Don't touch it."

Ten minutes later, the police come. They look at the bag.

"Everybody, please listen! There is a bag with no owner. It is dangerous. Please leave the library."

Everyone is shocked. They all leave the library. Emma and Gillian stay in the library. There are two police officers, and two men wearing special suits.

"Why are they wearing special suits?" Gillian asks a policewoman.

"Because they are from the bomb department," says the policewoman.

"Do you think there is a bomb in the bag?" asks Gillian.

"Maybe," says the policewoman. "Did you see anyone strange in the library today?"

"No, I didn't," says Gillian. "How about you, Emma?"

"I was in my office most of the day. I didn't see anything," says Emma.

"OK, please go outside," says the policewoman. "It is too dangerous in here."

Emma and Gillian go outside. There are many people outside. There are two police vans and a police car. Some people are taking videos on their smartphones.

When they see Emma and Gillian, they ask questions.

"What is happening?"

"Is there a bomb?"

"Is it dangerous?"

"We don't know," says Emma.

Then, a TV reporter and a cameraman come.

"Excuse me, can we interview you?" the reporter asks Emma.

Emma is surprised. But she says, "OK."

Inside the library, the police officers wearing special clothes go near the bag.

"Be careful. Move it slowly," says one of the police officers.

One of the police officers touches the bag.

"There is something hard inside it," he says. "Let's use the robot to open the bag."

The police send a robot to open the bag. The robot opens it.

Then, the policemen walk to the bag very slowly. One of the policemen looks inside the bag. "Potatoes and carrots!" he says. "It isn't a bomb! It's potatoes and carrots!"

Outside the library, Gillian sees Fred. He is walking to the library. He looks worried.

"What is happening?" he asks.

"The police think there is a bomb in the library," says Gillian.

"A bomb? That's terrible!" says Fred. "I came back because I left my shopping bag here."

Gillian looks at him. "You left your shopping bag?" she asks. "What was inside it?"

"Potatoes and carrots!" says Fred.

4. THE CLOTHES SHOP

Nick is in the back room of his clothes shop.

This is strange, he thinks. *Yesterday, there were ten sweaters here. Now, there are only seven.*

He looks at the T-shirts. *And yesterday, there were twenty T-shirts. Now, there are only fifteen. Someone is taking clothes from here.*

Nick goes out of the back room and closes the door. Veronica is working in the store today. She is helping a customer. Nick looks at her.

I have two workers, he thinks. *Veronica and Sarah. They are both good workers. I don't think they will take clothes from the back room. Maybe it is a customer. I don't lock the back room.*

Some more customers come into the shop, and Nick helps them. At 5:00pm, the shop closes.

"I'm going home now," says Veronica. "I'll see you tomorrow."

"OK, see you tomorrow, Veronica," says Nick.

Veronica goes into the back room. She takes her coat and goes out of the shop.

Maybe I need a security camera, thinks Nick. *I'll order one online.*

Nick orders a security camera online. He finishes work at 7:00pm.

Two days later, the camera comes. Nick puts the camera in the back room when Sarah is on her lunch break. The shop is busy today. Nick has no time to think about the camera. At 5:00pm, Sarah goes home. Nick checks the camera data on his phone. He sees Sarah go into the back room and pick up her coat. Then, she goes out of the back room.

No customers enter the back room. He goes into the back room and checks the clothes. There is no problem.

The next day, Veronica is working. Nick and Veronica have a busy day. At 5:00pm, Veronica goes home. Nick checks the camera data on his phone.

"What?" he is very shocked. When Veronica picked up her coat, she took three T-shirts and put them in her bag.

"It's Veronica!" he says. "She is taking clothes from my shop!"

Nick thinks about the problem. *I will talk to Veronica tomorrow,* he thinks.

The next day, Veronica comes to work.

"Good morning, Nick. How are you today?" she asks.

"I'm OK, but I want to talk to you," says Nick.

"OK. I'll take my coat off," says Veronica. She goes into the back room and takes her coat off. Nick goes into the back room.

"Veronica, look at this," he says. He shows her the camera data. Veronica starts to cry.

"I'm sorry," she says.

"You are taking clothes from here. I trusted you. You are a good worker. But you take clothes from my shop. I'm going to call the police."

"No! Please don't call the police!" says Veronica. "I will explain."

Veronica is crying loudly. "I have three children. My husband lost his job a month ago. We have no money. I get money from my job here, but it is not much. My children are hungry. I want to buy food for my family. So, I take clothes from here, and sell them online."

"What? You sell them online?" Nick is shocked.

"Yes. And then I can buy food to feed my children. I'm so sorry, Nick. I won't do it again. Please don't call the police."

Nick thinks about the problem. *Veronica and her husband have no money. So Veronica took the clothes. She did a bad thing. If I call the police, she will have more problems. But I can't forgive her.*

"OK, Veronica. I won't tell the police," he says.

"Oh thank you!" says Veronica.

"But I can't trust you anymore. So, you can't work here. I'm sorry. Please look for a new job."

Veronica looks sad, but she says, "OK."

She picks up her coat. "I'll go to the job centre," she says. "If the job centre calls you, will you tell them about this?"

"No," says Nick. "It is our secret. You need money for your family. I understand. But you did a bad thing."

Veronica says, "I'm sorry." Then, she goes out of the back room and out of the shop.

This is a sad situation, thinks Nick. *I like Veronica. She was a good worker. But I can't forgive her for taking the clothes. I hope she and her husband find good jobs. Now, I need to find new staff.*

5. THE JEWELLERY SHOP

Eric is in the jewellery shop. He is looking for a birthday present for his wife. She will be 65 years old next week.

Dave owns the jewellery shop. He knows Eric very well. Eric is famous in Glasstown. Thirty years ago, he was the town's best rugby player. He played for the national team.

"How about a necklace for Elizabeth?" asks Dave.

"Hmm. I bought her a necklace last year. Maybe this year I will buy a bracelet," says Eric.

"There are some bracelets here," says Dave. Eric and Dave look at the bracelets in the glass counter.

Then, there is a loud noise outside. It is a motorbike. Dave and Eric look outside. A man wearing a black mask runs into the shop. He has a hammer and a gun.

"Give me the jewellery!" he shouts. He points the gun at Dave. He starts to break the glass counter with the hammer.

Dave is very shocked, but Eric is not shocked. He is angry. He is 65 years old, but he is very big and strong. He puts his arms around the man's legs. It is a rugby tackle. The man falls on the floor. Then, Eric sits on the man and punches him in the face.

"Ouch! That hurt!" shouts the man.

Eric is shouting at Dave. "Call the police! Call the police!"

Two young men outside the shop hear the noise. They look inside. Then, they see the motorbike.

"The man inside the shop is trying to take jewellery! He has a gun! And this man on the motorbike is waiting for him!" says one of the men. "Let's get him!"

The man on the motorbike tries to escape, but the two young men hit him. He falls off the motorbike. The two men sit on the man. Many people are watching. Some other people go into the shop and help Eric.

Soon, the police come. They take the man from the shop and the man on the motorbike.

People go into the shop. "Are you OK, Dave?" they ask.

"Yes, I'm fine. Eric is a hero," says Dave. He rugby tackled the man with the gun.

"I'm not a hero," says Eric. "I just want to buy a present for my wife."

Some other police officers come into the shop. They ask Dave and Eric for information. They also want to check the shop security cameras.

About thirty minutes later, a newspaper reporter and cameraman come into the shop. The reporter interviews Eric and Dave, and the cameraman takes pictures.

"Would you like to say anything?" the reporter asks Dave.

"Yes," says Dave. "Glasstown is a famous rugby town. All the men in the town practice rugby at school. And Eric here is a famous rugby player. So, if you want to rob shops in this town, you will have trouble! The jewellery robbers picked the wrong town!"

THANK YOU

Thank you for reading Around Town. We hope you enjoyed the stories. (Word count: 3,585)

If you would like to read more graded readers, please visit our website http://www.italkyoutalk.com

Other Level 1 graded readers include
A Business Trip to New York
Adventure on the Mountain
A Homestay in Auckland
A Trip to London
Dear Ellen
Emily's Bag
Everyday Heroes
Haruna's Story Part 1
Haruna's Story Part 2
Haruna's Story Part 3
Jimmy Luther
Ken's Story Part 1
Ken's Story Part 2
Life is Surprising!
Phil's Balloon
Saori and the Storm
Strange Stories
The Christmas Present

ABOUT THE AUTHOR

I Talk You Talk Press is an award-winning Japan-based publisher of language textbooks, graded readers and language learning/teaching resources. We won the Language Learner Literature Award in 2019 and 2020.

Our team is made up of highly experienced language teachers and translators, who have all studied at least one additional language to an advanced level.

This experience enables us to design our materials from the perspective of both the teacher and the learner. We consult with both teachers and language learners when designing our textbooks and graded readers, and test our materials extensively in the classroom before publication.

We are a fast-growing press, and currently publish graded readers for learners of English. We publish new graded readers monthly.

Around Town

Around Town

www.ingramcontent.com/pod-product-compliance
Lightning Source LLC
LaVergne TN
LVHW042241190726
843491LV00003BA/1176